THE GREATEST RECORDS IN SPORTS

BASEBALL'S
GREATEST RECORDS

D1736547

Andrew Pina

PowerKiDS
press

New York

Published in 2015 by The Rosen Publishing Group, Inc.
29 East 21st Street, New York, NY 10010

First Edition

Editor: Katie Kawa
Book Design: Reann Nye

Photo Credits: Cover (baseball diamond) mirounga/Shutterstock.com; cover (Greg Maddux) Mitchell Layton/Getty Images Sport/Getty Images; cover (Rickey Henderson) Brad Mangin/ Sports Illustrated/Getty Images; p. 5 Aspen Photo/Shutterstock.com; p. 7 B Bennett/Getty Images Sport/ Getty Images; p. 9 Hulton Archive/Getty Images; p. 11 Takeo Tanuma/Sports Illustrated/Getty Images; p. 13 John G. Zimmerman/Sports Illustrated/Getty Images; p. 14 General Photographic Agency/ Hulton Archive/Getty Images; p. 15 Al Messerschmidt/Getty Images Sport/Getty Images; p. 17 The Sporting News/Sporting News/Getty Images; p. 18 Jerry Wachter/Sports Illustrated/ Getty Images; p. 19 Lisa Blumenfeld/Getty Images Sport/Getty Images; p. 21 Rick Stewart/ Getty Images Sport/Getty Images; p. 23 Focus On Sport/Getty Images; p. 25 Robert Riger/Getty Images Sport/Getty Images; p. 26 Photo File/Hulton Archive/Getty Images; p. 27 TED MATHIAS/AFP/ Getty Images; p. 29 Vincent Laforet/Getty Images Sport/Getty Images; p. 30 Al Bello/ Getty Images Sport/Getty Images.

Library of Congress Cataloging-in-Publication Data

Pina, Andrew.
Baseball's greatest records / by Andrew Pina.
p. cm. — (The greatest records in sports)
Includes index.
ISBN 978-1-4994-0235-3 (pbk.)
ISBN 978-1-4994-0184-4 (6-pack)
ISBN 978-1-4994-0230-8 (library binding)
1. Baseball — Records — United States — Juvenile literature. I. Pina, Andrew. II. Title.
GV877.P57 2015
796.357—d23

Manufactured in the United States of America

CPSIA Compliance Information: Batch #CW15PK: For Further Information contact Rosen Publishing, New York, New York at 1-800-237-9932

CONTENTS

Baseball has been played for a long time. Early forms of baseball were played as far back as the 1700s. **Professional** baseball started in the late 1860s, just after the Civil War. That's when people began recording **statistics**, or stats. Stats are used to figure out who holds the greatest records in baseball's long history. Some records last for a short time, but some records are over 100 years old and may never be broken.

Some older records were set before 1920. During this time, very few home runs were hit, pitchers threw for many more innings, and some rules were different. Modern baseball, which is the sport as we know it today, began in 1920.

The best players in baseball history are **inducted** into the Baseball Hall of Fame, which is in Cooperstown, New York.

AMERICAN LEAGUE AND NATIONAL LEAGUE

The highest level of professional baseball in the United States is Major League Baseball (MLB). It has two leagues—the American League and the National League. MLB records cover both leagues, but each league also keeps its own records. **Awards** such as the Gold Glove are given to players in both leagues each year.

HITS AND BATTING AVERAGE

A hit is a stat recorded when a player hits the ball and safely gets to a base. Batting average is the **percentage** of total **at bats** that end with a hit.

It's not easy to get a hit. Every player who's ever played baseball has failed to get a hit more times than they've gotten a hit. Getting a hit 30 percent of the time is very good. Ted Williams was the last player to get a hit 40 percent of the time in a single season, and that happened in 1941.

Ichiro Suzuki is one of the greatest hitters ever. In 2001, after playing eight seasons in Japan, Ichiro was the first position player—or a player other than a pitcher—from that country to join the MLB. Three years later, he broke the 84-year-old single-season hit record, getting 262 hits.

SUPERIOR STATS
MOST CAREER HITS

PLAYER	HITS
PETE ROSE	4,256
TY COBB	4,189
HANK AARON	3,771
STAN MUSIAL	3,630
TRIS SPEAKER	3,514

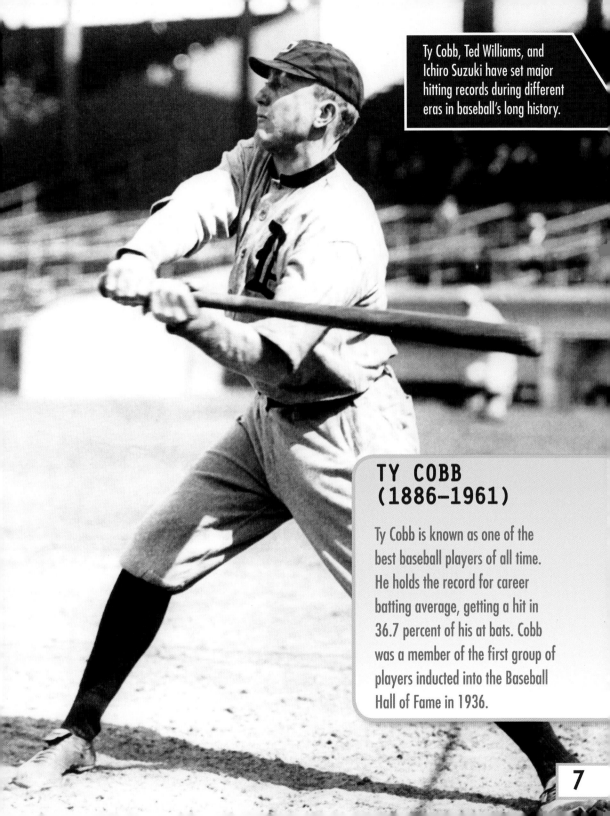

Ty Cobb, Ted Williams, and Ichiro Suzuki have set major hitting records during different eras in baseball's long history.

TY COBB
(1886–1961)

Ty Cobb is known as one of the best baseball players of all time. He holds the record for career batting average, getting a hit in 36.7 percent of his at bats. Cobb was a member of the first group of players inducted into the Baseball Hall of Fame in 1936.

In 1941, Joe DiMaggio had the longest hitting **streak** in baseball history. DiMaggio, an outfielder for the New York Yankees, had at least one hit in 56 **consecutive** games. The streak began on May 15 and ended on July 17.

DiMaggio didn't have to get a hit in every at bat, but he needed one hit in every game. In 34 games, he only had one hit, but that was all he needed to keep the streak going. He had 91 hits and 15 home runs in those 56 games.

Since DiMaggio set the record, only one player, Pete Rose, has even had a 40-game hit streak. Many believe DiMaggio's record hitting streak will never be matched.

SUPERIOR STATS
LONGEST HITTING STREAKS

PLAYER	CONSECUTIVE GAMES WITH A HIT	SEASON
JOE DIMAGGIO	56	1941
WILLIE KEELER	45	1896–1897
PETE ROSE	44	1978
BILL DAHLEN	42	1894
GEORGE SISLER	41	1922

DiMaggio got his nickname, "Joltin' Joe," from a song that was written about his famous hitting streak.

JOE DIMAGGIO
(1914–1999)

Joe DiMaggio's hitting streak is considered by many to be one of baseball's unbeatable records. Two years after his streak came to an end, he joined the U.S. Army to serve during World War II. In 1946, DiMaggio returned to the Yankees. He was inducted into the Baseball Hall of Fame in 1955.

HOME RUNS

Home runs are one of the most exciting parts of any baseball game. A home run happens when a ball is hit so far that it goes over the fence. The batter touches all the bases to score a run, and anyone else on base also scores a run.

Sometimes a batter will hit the ball inside the park, but still run all the way around the bases to score a run. This is called an inside-the-park home run.

Many home run records were set in the 1990s and early 2000s, during what's been called the **steroid** era. Some record holders admitted to using steroids or were believed to have used them. Steroids aren't allowed by MLB, but the league didn't test for their presence in players' bodies until 2004.

SUPERIOR STATS
MOST MLB CAREER HOME RUNS

PLAYER	HOME RUNS
BARRY BONDS	762
HANK AARON	755
BABE RUTH	714
WILLIE MAYS	660
ALEX RODRIGUEZ*	654

* = active player

SADAHARU OH
(1940–)

Baseball is played all over the world, and Japan has one of the world's best leagues. The world record holder for home runs is a Japanese player, Sadaharu Oh. Playing for the Yomiuri Giants, Oh hit 868 home runs during his career. That's 106 more than Barry Bonds!

Hank Aaron

Sadaharu Oh

In 1974, Hank Aaron was the greatest home run hitter in the United States, and Sadaharu Oh was the greatest in Japan. They faced each other in a home run contest in Tokyo, which Aaron won 10–9.

OTHER HITTING RECORDS

Hitting isn't just about knocking the ball over the fence. Many players work hard to be good all-around hitters. On-base percentage (OBP) and slugging percentage are two stats that help show how good a hitter is.

OBP is the percentage of times a player gets to a base, divided by their total number of plate appearances. A plate appearance is any time a batter steps up to home plate to try to get on base. The three ways to reach a base, which increase OBP, are a hit, a walk, and a hit-by-pitch. A walk occurs when a pitcher throws four balls, which are pitches outside of a batter's **strike zone**. The batter has to be smart enough not to swing at those pitches.

TED WILLIAMS (1918–2002)

Ted Williams, who played outfield for the Boston Red Sox, holds the record for best career OBP. Williams served his country in the military during World War II, taking time away from the Red Sox to do so. He was inducted into the Baseball Hall of Fame in 1966.

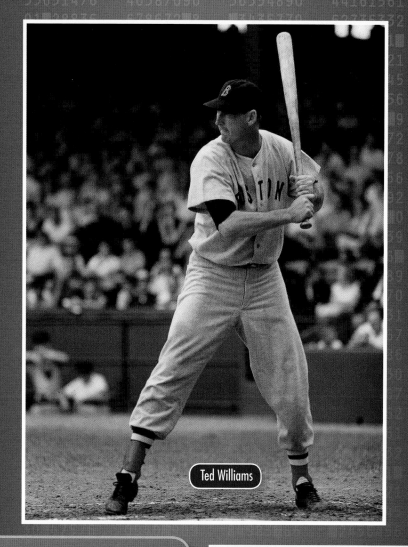
Ted Williams

SUPERIOR STATS
HIGHEST CAREER OBP

PLAYER	OBP
TED WILLIAMS	.482
BABE RUTH	.474
JOHN MCGRAW	.466
BILLY HAMILTON	.455
LOU GEHRIG	.447

OBP is shown using decimals, but it's still a percentage. For example, Ted Williams's career OBP of .482 means that 48.2 percent of his plate appearances ended with him getting on base.

Slugging percentage measures how many total bases a player gets per at bat. Slugging percentage is a good way to show how powerful a hitter is.

The number of bases a batter touches after an at bat is measured in total bases. A single gets one total base, a double gets two total bases, a triple get three total bases, and a home run gets four total bases. An out gets zero bases. The total bases are divided by the number of at bats to find a player's slugging percentage.

BABE RUTH
(1895–1948)

George Herman Ruth had many nicknames: the Great Bambino, the Sultan of Swat, and of course, Babe. Early in his career, Ruth was a pitcher and a hitter. Later, he stopped pitching and played in the outfield. In 1927, Ruth hit 60 home runs. This was a single-season record that stood until Roger Maris broke it in 1961.

Ruth joined Ty Cobb, Honus Wagner, Christy Mathewson, and Walter Johnson as the first players to be inducted into the Baseball Hall of Fame in 1936.

Babe Ruth and Ted Williams hold the top two places in both OBP and slugging percentage. Williams leads in OBP, and Ruth leads in slugging. Both players were feared hitters in their day. They combined great awareness of the strike zone with powerful home run swings.

SUPERIOR STATS
HIGHEST CAREER
SLUGGING PERCENTAGE

PLAYER	SLUGGING PERCENTAGE
BABE RUTH	.690
TED WILLIAMS	.634
LOU GEHRIG	.632
JIMMIE FOXX	.609
BARRY BONDS	.607

If a runner on base runs to the next base while the pitcher is about to pitch, it's called a stolen base. Base stealers have to be very fast. They need to make it to the next base before the catcher or pitcher throws the ball to an infielder who can tag them and make an out. Players can steal second base, third base, or even home plate! They often slide into the bases to avoid being tagged with the ball.

The rules for stealing bases were very different before 1898, so stats from that time period can't be compared to modern base-stealing stats. The record for most stolen bases since 1898 is held by Rickey Henderson. He stole 1,406 bases in his career.

SUPERIOR STATS
MOST STOLEN BASES IN A CAREER

PLAYER	STEALS
RICKEY HENDERSON	1,406
LOU BROCK	938
BILLY HAMILTON	914
TY COBB	897
TIM RAINES	808

Henderson set the modern MLB record for single-season steals in 1982. During that season, he stole 130 bases!

RICKEY HENDERSON
(1958–)

The greatest base stealer of all time is Rickey Henderson. He stole 100 bases or more in three different seasons. He played for 25 seasons, which helped him record so many steals. Henderson was inducted into the Baseball Hall of Fame in 2009.

Both the American and the National Leagues present the Gold Glove to the best fielder at each position each season. Managers, coaches, and baseball **researchers** vote to decide who gets the award.

Fielding is very important, and it takes different skills to play different fielding positions. Infielders need quick **reflexes** and an **accurate** arm. Outfielders need to be fast and have a strong arm. Catchers need to have a very strong and accurate arm to throw out base stealers.

OZZIE SMITH
(1954–)

Shortstop Ozzie Smith, nicknamed the "Wizard of Oz," won 13 Gold Gloves. That's the record for most Gold Gloves for his position. Shortstop is a difficult position to play because more balls are hit to this position than any other on the field. Smith was known to celebrate on the field with backflips!

Both Maddux and Smith are members of the Baseball Hall of Fame.

Greg Maddux

The player with the most career Gold Gloves is a pitcher, Greg Maddux. Maddux had very quick reflexes. He finished his pitches facing the plate with his feet pointing at the batter, so he was always ready if the ball was hit to him.

SUPERIOR STATS
MOST CAREER GOLD GLOVES

PLAYER	POSITION	GOLD GLOVES
GREG MADDUX	PITCHER	18
BROOKS ROBINSON	THIRD BASE	16
JIM KAAT	PITCHER	16
OZZIE SMITH	SHORTSTOP	13
IVAN RODRIGUEZ	CATCHER	13

"Strike three!" That's what a pitcher wants to hear at the end of every at bat. A strike is when the batter swings and misses a pitch or doesn't swing at a pitch in their strike zone. Three strikes equal a strikeout. A strikeout is one way to get an out in a baseball game, and after three outs, it's the fielding team's turn to bat again.

Nolan Ryan was one of the most feared pitchers of all time. His most famous pitch was his fastball, which earned him the nickname the "Ryan Express," because there was only one stop—the catcher's mitt.

SUPERIOR STATS
MOST CAREER STRIKEOUTS

PLAYER	STRIKEOUTS
NOLAN RYAN	5,714
RANDY JOHNSON	4,875
ROGER CLEMENS	4,672
STEVE CARLTON	4,136
BERT BLYLEVEN	3,701

Ryan's pitches could reach speeds of nearly 100 miles (161 km) per hour!

Ryan's MLB career lasted for 27 seasons. His lengthy career—combined with his unstoppable fastball—helped him collect the most strikeouts ever (5,714). No other pitcher has even made it to 5,000 strikeouts!

NOLAN RYAN
(1947–)

In 1973, Nolan Ryan set the modern MLB record for most strikeouts in a season, with 383. During his long MLB career, Ryan struck out 1,176 different batters! He was inducted into the Baseball Hall of Fame in 1999 because of his many pitching records, including most career strikeouts.

The best game a pitcher can have is a no-hitter. In a no-hitter, the pitcher throws the whole game without allowing a hit. However, a batter can still reach bases on walks, fielding mistakes (known as errors), or getting hit by a pitch. To throw a no-hitter, a pitcher generally needs to throw a lot of strikes. Nolan Ryan had many strikeouts to help him record seven no-hitters, the most ever.

No-hitters are a big accomplishment for a pitcher and their whole team. Many times, a fielder will make a great play, such as a diving catch, to help preserve the no-hitter. No-hitters are very rare, so they're celebrated by both players and fans when they happen.

SUPERIOR STATS
MOST CAREER NO-HITTERS

PLAYER	NO-HITTERS
NOLAN RYAN	7
SANDY KOUFAX	4
LARRY CORCORAN	3
BOB FELLER	3
CY YOUNG	3

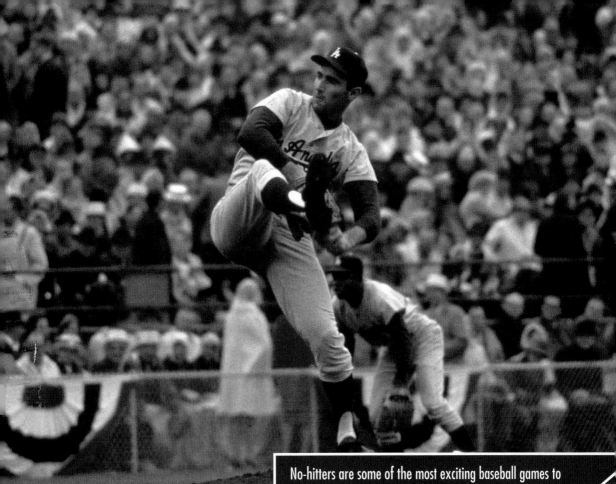

No-hitters are some of the most exciting baseball games to watch. Sandy Koufax threw four no-hitters, and his last one was a perfect game!

A PERFECT GAME

A perfect game is a special kind of no-hitter, in which the pitcher doesn't allow any players to reach base — not by a hit, a walk, or an error. No one has thrown more than one perfect game. Even though Nolan Ryan threw seven no-hitters, he never threw a perfect game.

SCORELESS INNING STREAKS

No pitcher wants to let a runner score a run. If a pitcher doesn't allow a run over a nine-inning game, it's called a shutout. Warren Spahn holds the modern baseball record for most career shutouts, with 63. All the pitchers ahead of him on the career shutout list played in the late 1800s and early 1900s. Spahn played from 1942 to 1965.

Orel Hershiser of the Los Angeles Dodgers holds the record for most consecutive scoreless innings, with 59 in 1988. He broke the record of fellow Dodger Don Drysdale, who pitched 58 scoreless innings in a row in 1968.

SUPERIOR STATS
LONGEST SCORELESS INNING STREAKS

PLAYER	SEASON	CONSECUTIVE SCORELESS INNINGS
OREL HERSHISER	1988	59
DON DRYSDALE	1968	58
WALTER JOHNSON	1913	55.2
JACK COOMBS	1910	53
BOB GIBSON	1968	47

CY YOUNG AWARD

The year Hershiser set the scoreless innings streak record, he won the Cy Young Award. The American League and the National League both give this award to the best pitcher each season, as voted by baseball writers. Roger Clemens holds the record for most career Cy Young Awards, with seven.

Like Joe DiMaggio's hitting streak, Hershiser's scoreless inning streak is a baseball record no one has come close to breaking since it was set.

Many people think this record is unbreakable. Since the record was set, only one pitcher, Arizona Diamondback Brandon Webb, has even had a 40-inning streak. Webb threw 42 consecutive scoreless innings in 2007.

It's important to show up for work every day. Cal Ripken Jr. took this belief to heart. He played in 2,632 consecutive games, which is the most in baseball history. Ripken, who played for his hometown Baltimore Orioles for his whole career, didn't miss a game in more than 16 straight seasons.

Ripken broke the record that had been held by Lou Gehrig since 1939. Gehrig played in 2,130 straight games, which many thought was an unbreakable record. However, Ripken ended up playing in over 500 more consecutive games than Gehrig!

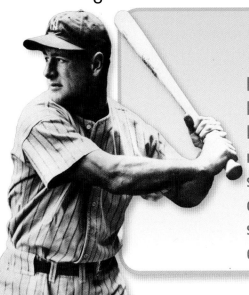

LOU GEHRIG
(1903–1941)

Henry Louis Gehrig was known as Lou and was nicknamed the Iron Horse. He might have played in even more consecutive games, but had to suddenly stop playing baseball because of a disease that affects the brain and spinal cord. It's now commonly known as Lou Gehrig's Disease.

Cal Ripken Jr.

Ripken joined Gehrig as a member of the Baseball Hall of Fame in 2007.

To play in that many games, for that long, you have to be a good player. During Ripken's streak, he won Rookie of the Year and two Most Valuable Player (MVP) awards. He also won a championship with the Orioles in 1983.

SUPERIOR STATS
MOST CONSECUTIVE GAMES PLAYED

PLAYER	GAMES PLAYED
CAL RIPKEN JR.	2,632
LOU GEHRIG	2,130
EVERETT SCOTT	1,307
STEVE GARVEY	1,207
MIGUEL TEJADA	1,152

Every MLB player wants his team to win the World Series, which is the league's championship. Every October, the best team in the American League plays the best team in the National League in the World Series. The teams play up to seven games, and the first team to win four is the World Series champion.

The New York Yankees have won 27 World Series championships, more than any other team in baseball. They won their first World Series in 1923, with Lou Gehrig and Babe Ruth. The Yankees won four straight championships from 1936 to 1939, as well as five straight from 1949 to 1953. They also won three championships in a row from 1998 to 2000, with star players such as Derek Jeter and Mariano Rivera.

MARIANO RIVERA
(1969–)

Mariano Rivera was a relief pitcher for the Yankees, and he holds the record for most career saves, with 652. A relief pitcher records a save when he finishes a close game that he didn't start and his team wins. Rivera won five World Series championships with the Yankees before he retired in 2013.

Mariano Rivera

The number of World Series championships a team has could change with each new season. Players have to be at their best to help their team win in October!

SUPERIOR STATS
MOST WORLD SERIES CHAMPIONSHIPS

TEAM	CHAMPIONSHIPS
NEW YORK YANKEES	27
ST. LOUIS CARDINALS	11
BOSTON RED SOX	8
SAN FRANCISCO/NEW YORK GIANTS	7
LOS ANGELES/BROOKLYN DODGERS	6

There are many more baseball records out there to discover. You can explore baseball history for yourself to find out more of baseball's greatest records. You could even visit the Baseball Hall of Fame to learn more about the most famous record holders in the sport. These record holders paved the way for the star players of today and tomorrow.

Derek Jeter

GLOSSARY

accurate: Capable of or successful in reaching an intended target.

at bat: An attempt to bat in baseball that does not count if the player walks, is hit by a pitch, is interfered with by the catcher, or makes a sacrifice play.

award: A prize given for doing something well.

consecutive: Following each other without interruption.

induct: To admit or bring in as a member.

percentage: Part of a whole.

professional: Having to do with a job someone does for a living.

reflex: An action or movement of the body that happens automatically as a reaction to something.

researcher: A person whose job is to study a subject deeply.

statistic: A number that stands for a piece of information.

steroid: A drug that is sometimes used illegally by athletes to help them become stronger and more muscular.

streak: A period of repeated success.

strike zone: The area over home plate through which a pitch must pass in order to be called a strike.

INDEX

WEBSITES

Due to the changing nature of Internet links, PowerKids Press has developed an online list of websites related to the subject of this book. This site is updated regularly. Please use this link to access the list: www.powerkidslinks.com/gris/base